THE
PARADOX
OF
SUFFERING

THE

PARADOX

OF

SUFFERING

The Voice of A Nurse

DELIA TUOTI FERRANDINO RN

XULON PRESS

Xulon Press
2301 Lucien Way #415
Maitland, FL 32751
407.339.4217
www.xulonpress.com

Paperback ISBN-13: 978-1-66283-719-7
Ebook ISBN-13: 978-1-66283-720-3

THE PARADOX OF SUFFERING

An Abstract of

A Thesis

Presented to the Graduate Faculty of W.C.S.U

By

Delia T. Ferrandino

In Partial Fulfillment

Of the Requirements for the Degree

Master of Arts

In English

Thesis Advisor

Dean of Arts and Sciences

_____

Date of Acceptance

TABLE OF CONTENTS

SUFFERING AND JOY

Acknowledgments

THE GENESIS OF this Master of Arts degree in English began with Dr. Daniel Joynt's suggestion that I apply for this degree. Without that first discussion, I would not be in my present situation. My creative germ was unintentionally guided at a time when I read Dr. John Brigg's text, *The Fire and the Crucible*. From that point forward, I took a class from Dr. Briggs on Virginia Woolf, and my creative flow never stopped, regardless of the many roadblocks in my life.

Dr. Ingrid Pruss had an early impact on my voice; she guided its cultivation. Dr. Karen Jambeck imparted the meticulous labor involved in editing numerous drafts. Dr. Oscar de los Santos inspired me to write in the middle of life's chaos.

I also thank my little girls, Clare and Elizabeth. These two incredible children frequently removed my fingers from the keyboard so that I might play with them. My frustration to be with them while I attended to multiple drafts gave my paper rich intertextuality. My sons, Jason and Stephen, were not only my first readers, but they were also the only people who could readily teach me how to use the computer. Their father, Mark, financially supported my dream.

Finally, I am grateful for an incredible man who befriended me during the final stages. Dr. David Buckley, professor of history, a constant friend and advisor, has never been unavailable for support.

Abstract

THIS THESIS IS a creative writing piece in fulfillment of the MA in English. It is a collection of five essays arranged in chronological order, according to my developing sense of suffering.

The first essay, "My Father's Funeral," explores my early experience with suffering and the need to survive loss. Writing this piece enabled me to see a common thread for connecting the following stories to one theme.

During the draft of the second essay, "The Tree House," a juvenile diabetic taught me that one can suffer in the midst of childhood. I became aware of one's nuances and the art of connecting them to my memory. I remember Saul's actions eclipsed his unspoken pain.

In the third essay, "Faded Photographs," I memorized my relatives' nuances as a way of remembering their presence. Observing details allowed me to survive my relatives' deaths.

In the fourth essay, "Pain," I relive my first experience as a nurse while giving care to a burn victim. While not making light of my patient's suffering, I recalled pleasant nuances as a way to endure the sight of Joe's agony. I found creative ways of perceiving joy within suffering.

The final essay, "Elizabeth's Story," could not have been written with any insight had I not experienced my father's funeral. While writing this piece about my mentally-challenged daughter, I kept thinking about the impact that one person has upon the other. This essay explores an opportunity to perceive disability with a new insight: what Elizabeth does have is the ability to unconditionally love others.

Introduction

LIKE THE ARTIST who carefully placed a series of black-and-white photographs on the gallery wall, I have mounted here for the reader selected pictures of events in my life and worked them into the form of personal essays. I have written these essays according to a single theme, and placed them in relation to an insight gained over the years: joy and sorrow can be found within each other.

The first piece in this sequence has special importance; it becomes the genesis of the next essay. That, in turn, leads to the third, and so on. In this crescendo of singular moments, the last essay, "Elizabeth's Story," turns into the final exposition of my thesis—that joy comes sometimes from the act of surviving. My life has been a mélange of the lives that have surrounded me. All life is important because each of us is the culmination of what we observe about others. After writing about these experiences, I now understand suffering is a perspective from which to observe another's patience, dignity, and love.

*"You will suffer, but in the suffering,
you will find joy in truth"*

My mother, _____

My Father's Funeral

An English professor once told me: "Your eyes have a revealing mystery about them, as if they carry the vision of a dark tragedy that they once viewed." I was not only startled by the observation, but I felt my privacy had been violated. After all, it had taken me a lifetime to cover my unhappiness with a mask of busy contentment. Coming and going, doing, and being all things to all people, I never suspected that anyone would actually see my saddened spirit. My eyes had seen something tragic.

I was eight years old the year that my father's doctors explained to him that there was no cure for prostate cancer. Shortly after hearing the news, he committed suicide.

On the day of the funeral, mother dressed us in woolen suits: mine was grey with black trim, and my sister's was navy blue with red trim. High, white-banded blouses covered our necks, and our suits featured silver metal buttons and a draped silver chain: all of these details created a Tyrolean, military appearance. We looked like stoic, somber soldiers about to mark a significant time. This look was fitting, for Mother always said, "Keep your chin up when you're feeling down, and go forward. There is a light at the end of every dark tunnel." I held my head up, but I felt my throat tightening as if it were girding itself against a tidal wave of emotions that might have engulfed us all. Silently, I marched forward toward the long, black car.

Lined up in front of the church were our friends, relatives, and Dad's business associates, as well as members of the community. Standing inside the nave of Saint Mary's Catholic Church, I felt embarrassed. Who were these people, and why were they here gawking at our personal misery? I felt like a monkey in a cage. Back in the car, I wiped away my tears and held back the urge to vomit. I resolved to keep others from noticing my internal hell; I decided I needed to not only look like a stoic soldier, but to feel like one. After all, even though they may have been invited guests, they did not have the right to intrude on my emotions. Even grief has its pride.

As we marched into the sanctuary, I was overcome by the dense scent of frankincense encircling my lowered head. I quickly caught a glimpse of my father lying in the casket. His white face bore no resemblance to the healthy tan he once had. Feeling my gut ripped open by the reality of death, I looked upward to escape this sight. Above were the broad, wood beams that supported the main church. Nestled between the walls and the beams were five luminous, stained-glass windows. The light that shone behind them cast clear, colored images of the saints. The images interrupted my grief and gave me a new choice: I did not want to stare at the incomprehensible situation of my father lying in a plush casket, looking like he was alive. Somehow the pictures on the glass gave a hint of hope, whereas the sight of my father did not.

He was in a cherry casket. He was dressed in the grey suit he had worn to his Rotary meeting the night before his suicide. I noticed his white shirt in stark contrast to the redness of his tie. The two colors seemed intensely bright, even though they began to bleed into each other. Just then I blinked. Every sight became meaningful. The tiny white polka dots on his red tie reminded me of the first-fallen snows that my father and I twirled around in. My eyes soaked up the scene like a journalist collecting supporting facts. Every nuance betrayed his presence, yet every detail bellowed out his absence.

Suddenly from behind, I felt my mother gently prodding my shoulder. She was saying I had enough time. I turned around and saw a line of people waiting to pay their last respects. Defiantly I turned my back on them. He was mine, not theirs. I blocked them out and returned to my father. His eyes were closed. I hoped that he was just sleeping. I looked at his chest like a medical examiner seeking signs of life before the final pronouncement of death. I counted to sixty and nothing happened. I began to imagine that if I talked to him, he might sit up. I watched him for the last time so intensely that my eyes watered. At eight, I believed my thoughts would speak louder than words. I thought that if I asked him to wake up, he would. I touched his right hand, and I felt the distance between us. While my hand was warm and moving, his hand was cold and vacant. That coldness became the reality of death.

The priest lit the frankincense bowl, and the church filled with a warm, earthy aroma. My head started to ache, and my thoughts became distant. Swirling in a vortex of disbelief, emptiness, and hopelessness, my knees buckled under me as I stood up. I fainted.

I had managed to forget about this day and its unending sadness, until a professor found it in my eyes forty years later. Is it always so? Do we carry our history in our eyes, revealing in our gaze what was revealed to us? Or is it our sadness that spills out to the observer, while our happier memories remain contently inside? Why did this professor see the sadness and not the joy I once shared in this family of five? Surely my experiences of joy from our lively family life should have been equally accessible to my professor's vision.

Our family lived in Ridgefield, Connecticut, in a house on twenty acres where Dad ran his landscaping business. We had a nursery on the lower ten acres; our house was on the upper front ten acres. Evergreens sprawled down our winding driveway. Flowered shrubs dotted the front lawn and filled the air with an intoxicating aroma that perfumed every breeze that entered our house. Dad loved the beauty he found within nature and art; but the business of making money and dealing with profit wore him down. He was the president of the local Rotary Club and a member of the Ridgefield Board of Education. He was responsible for supporting five children and a wife. Somewhere in his life, he found time to develop a weakness for wine, and when he suffered from frequent bouts of melancholy, he tried to eradicate the misery by drinking in the late afternoon. He tried several kinds of treatment for alcoholism, but nothing worked.

In 1962, burdened by drink and a recently discovered, fatal diagnosis, he drove to the lower property and struggled with his life, and then he took life away. On a sunny day in April, just two days before my eighth birthday, in the middle of the apple blossoms, Dad slumped forward against the red steering wheel of his Studebaker. The garden hose that once made the trees live was the same hose that ended his life. He had chosen death from carbon monoxide poisoning, rather than from cancer.

When my sister and I walked home from the bus stop that day we found Mom crying on the phone. She said to us, "Daddy has gone to heaven." Overcome with dread, my sister and I immediately ran around the house looking for a room to enter. Holding hands, rushing to detach ourselves from the family we had known all our lives, we ran down the hallway as if hiding from fire above. We were acutely aware of danger. Our family had received an assault. We ran to his office in an attempt to find him sitting at his desk, writing his bills. We ran with desperate hope, dry mouths and flailing arms ripping through the air that seemed to hold us back from the vacant reality that would loom behind his closed door.

When we got there, we only saw the life of papers floating off the desk from the eerie wind rushing through his office window. We found emptiness in his office. His sudden absence magnified the importance of his constant presence. His voice was gone. Though physically imposing, it was his voice that always filled the house. Now that voice was silent, and that silence did not give us instructions. We stood still. The house stood still. The business stopped functioning. The daily coming and going of all the trucks and the workers anxiously awaiting their daily wages stood still. Oddly, the days continued to arrive in succession without a break, but it was no longer clear what we were to do with them.

Later, I recalled one evening in the last year of his life when my father took the time to read me a Dr. Seuss story. I loved to hear him read to me. On his lap, in the warmth of his sturdy arms, I began to rhyme out loud while my dad joined in. The words were nonsense, but they rhymed. He did not correct me because like me, he found music in the words. My mother walked by with an armful of laundry, and he remarked, "Our little girl is a poet." Our words became a spontaneous interchange of lyrical theatrics. Together, we enjoyed the wonder of the words as they vibrated in our throats.

Years later, I realized that by nurturing my fondness of literature, my father was investing a part of himself. He knew he would one day die, so he was leaving a part of himself that would live through me in spite of his absence.

"Happiness is a butterfly, which when pursued, is always just beyond your grasp, but which, if you will sit down quietly, may alight upon you."

Nathaniel Hawthorne

THE TREE HOUSE

I WAS NINE during the summer of 1963, when my eleven-year-old sister and I played in the tree house our sixteen-year-old brother had built. The crude house was a three-foot box fashioned out of plywood. It sat in the limbs of a majestic, two-hundred-year-old sugar maple. With its vibrant red, orange, and yellow leaves looming above its large trunk, the tree had main branches covered with bark that held a series of linear ripples resembling wide-wale corduroy. Rough to the touch, the texture made it easier to grab hold of the tree. Curiously enough, climbing down those branches was never quite as easy as climbing up, and at times, when I started to slip, there was the safety of two interlocking limbs that provided a built-in seat for resting. These spaces in between the tight branches made interesting nooks and crannies that allowed me to watch the sunlit leaves dazzle with spots of blinding, white, brightness.

At the bottom, by the exposed roots, was a succession of twelve narrow boards. Those were rungs of the ladder that led to the tree house. These steps led my sister and me up to the front door. Entering the narrow opening required some skill, for this passage was under the house, and I had to pull my weight up and over to sit beside the entrance. Once inside, Michele and I looked down at the neighborhood for what seemed like miles. We spied on neighborhood kids and soon realized that it would be more fun to share our hidden space with some friends. We invited two neighborhood brothers, Saul and Seth, who had just moved in from Long Island. They were different from us; they had an accent and wore dressy clothes; we on the other hand, did not have an accent (or so we thought), and Michele and I wore blue jeans and tee shirts. Saul was tall, thin, and dark eyed. His hair was cut like a bowl around his head where the bangs just touched his brows. Seth was younger and had curly light brown hair. Both of them seemed more like our brothers, and none of us talked about differences in gender. We were all interested in baseball, military figurines, and decorating our bikes for the Memorial Day Parade.

It was there, in between the space of the branches, that we all held discussions about cooking meals in the tree house. During crisp afternoons, we gathered household and camping supplies. Saul and Seth brought their parents' small, sterno-stove, and Michele and I brought canteens and mess kits. Together, we prepared *Lipton's* chicken noodle soup ceremoniously. One person opened the packet, the second stirred the mixture, and the third poured the warm, steamy liquid into Styrofoam cups. Then we all raised the cups to our lips and watched the steam form clouds of condensation about our faces. The warmth of the liquid against the cool autumn air was the cozy insulation against the cold reality we were about to witness. I was about to understand how to see a person. I was about to experience the way one's struggles might, in fact, be the way one experiences joy. Saul became our teacher.

Before we broke bread, Saul separated himself into a quiet, clinical act that he never spoke about. He silently performed a ritual every four hours. First, he opened a plastic cooler. Then he removed a glass vial, and withdrew twelve millimeters of cloudy insulin from a hypodermic needle. The vial was then placed back on the ice. Finally, without wincing, this calm, ten-year-old child rolled up his loose khaki pant leg, leaving a small patch of golden hairs exposed on his lean, left leg. With his right hand, he jammed the needled syringe into his skin. His hand dropped, and the pant leg rolled down like the tired lid of an eye that had seen too much, too soon. Then like an artist who gathers his brushes and paints with great care,

Saul put his supplies back into the bag. We all looked at him in awe, but we didn't know what to ask him. Saul's concentration prevented anyone from breaking his silence.

Despite his juvenile diabetic state, Saul played all the same games. His painful reality was right there in the center of our whimsical, healthy childhood, yet we had no clear idea that he was living in the midst of a debilitating disease. I was always caught up in his presiding presence that seemed to make our time together more complete. He was a member of our small community. We had to wait until Saul was done. He taught us that waiting comes before the expected joy. Saul's illness was not what we looked at. It was his deliberateness, his commitment to his actions, his quiet coming and going that influenced us. I developed a sense of looking at the nuances that make a person complete despite one's appearance. Those nuances help me remember someone long after time has passed.

Thirty years had gone by since we played in the tree house. One day, as I was leaving the Ridgefield Recreation Center, a shape caught my attention. At first it wasn't the figure, but the shadow behind the figure that became apparent. Then I turned and watched a fifty-year-old man sweeping the floor of this teen-center that we all had frequented in our youth. At first glance, I saw an indomitable spirit led by a healthy-looking body supported, not by flesh-covered legs, but by two metal shafts laced with white running shoes. I felt a pain rip through my chest, knowing the surgeries he had endured. This thin man was quietly graceful as he worked amidst his challenges. There was a slow, even temperament revealed within the methodical flow of his arms. His body, in excellent physical tone, seemed to be dancing with the mop. His mannerisms reminded me of someone I once knew.

Recognizing his face, I stopped him in the hallway saying, "Saul, I thought that was you." He smiled with a look of quiet content: he had this broad smile and bashful tilt of his head that spoke of fond memories—the memories of those days of climbing up the ladder to light matches had become the glimmer in his eyes. Neither of us had time to talk. We both smiled and turned away. I looked back at his receding form. I tried to hold on to a scene from those days in the tree house; all of us sitting still waiting for the sterno to boil the water while warm breezes brought butterflies that landed upon us.

Saul walked down the corridor on two steel shafts without wobbling hesitation, showing that while one may be born with a disability, it is one's indomitable spirit that the observer remembers. I walked away, wondering if the sight of Saul somehow gave me the insight to redefine disability. I began to think about the way people conduct themselves in the face of adversity, and I felt that while problems cannot be removed, they can be examples of courage for those yet to experience their own struggles.

"Buy me nothing; no books; they can't tell me any-thing as interesting as the things I've done. And since I don't have much time left, I don't want anything to distract me from my memories."

Marcel Proust

Faded Photographs

Past sights and sounds elicit an awareness of tradition and a sense of belonging. My childhood visits to our relative's home at 74 Walnut Street, in New Rochelle, New York, during the years from 1955 to 1971 became the memories that echo the significance of my life. As a solace, the nuances of my family tradition became a visible form of joy that I could inculcate into my wounded spirit, not only shortly after my eighth birthday and my father's death, but also into my adulthood.

Reflecting back to the time when I was nine, I remember my French grandmother, Sauline, had lived on the third floor of her brownstone apartment with my aunt Elvira and uncle Sal. My mother would drive me down from our home in Connecticut. When we got out of the car, my mother would ring the buzzer and wait for the door to release. From that moment on, it was like entering another world where nothing changed and expectations were always met: the freshly grated parmesan cheese scented the air with its musty aroma; the fresh green and purple grapes lined a cobalt-blue ceramic plate; and the oil paintings announcing Aunt Elvira's artistic talent hung on the plaster walls in the narrow hallway. There was a painting of an antique, apple press which she said was "your father's favorite."

There was that word, *f-a-t-h-e-r,* that signified so much, yet in reality had been spoken of so little since he died. I wondered what impact my father's death had upon his mother who was now before me. She was eighty, and he predeceased her. Even in her last years, she suffered. I wondered how she coped with disappointments. I looked for my relative's strength as a way of increasing my own courage to cope with my loss. I looked deeply around the room and tried to infuse its details into my mind so that I could retrieve some solace after we left there.

My grandmother radiated quiet wisdom, so there was nothing to do with her but to sit and revere her, as she sat in bed with long silver braids coiled on the crown of her head. Propped up by soft, lace pillows atop a feather comforter, she panned the room like an investigator looking for clues. I would sit on her bed waiting to hear a story, but she did not say much—she never did. She was one of those people who never let on what she was thinking. But I sensed both her lack of fear and anger. She appeared peaceful. Her eyes glimmered with an apparent understanding that gave me firm confidence. I sensed that whatever might happen in life, this woman had gone through it already and had made it through intact.

Grandmother, as a young widow, had raised five children: one son graduated from Harvard and my father graduated from Cornell, and Aunt Elvira won a full scholarship to the prestigious art college, Cooper Union. Somehow, sitting next to her gave me the reassurance that I might inherit her ability for endurance. I was comforted by her presence.

Then there was Uncle Sal, then seventy, bald and severely bent over. He often sat by the window, waiting to play Cat's Cradle with me. Until I joined him, he would watch the comings and goings of the neighbors on the sidewalks as attentively as he once watched his stocks crash. Disabled by the crippling effects of arthritis, it took all of his energy to entertain me on these visits. He waited for me to drop a loop so he could scoop me up in his arms and tickle me to exhaustion. I was always in a constant state of laughter and didn't quite know if Uncle Sal needed me to entertain him more than I needed him to entertain me. I always felt cherished by his attention and never wanted our time together to end.

Then, out of nowhere, Aunt Elvira would break our secret world of play to announce some annoying reality like serving lunch. Oh, but she put on quite an elegant show. This light meal was artistically prepared with the same attention that she gave to one of her paintings. She expected our full attention to her handiwork as if we were part of a gallery opening. It wasn't that the food was complex; quite honestly, lunch was elegantly simple. There was fresh parmesan cheese, Genoa salami, and crusty French bread served on a small, hand-painted plate. This small fare brought us all to the table rather ceremoniously. When we were all seated under the gaze of the artist, Uncle Sal would break the silence by pouring a small glass of red wine and seltzer water in a four-ounce jelly jar. Then he handed it to me with deliberate attention, as if to say that drinking wine was one of life's pleasures. As I sipped the special drink, my eyes would drift around the room, not really focusing on the adults anymore but on objects that I could imprint in my memory.

I sat there nervously nibbling the grapes and thinking how the cheese grater attached to the back of the pantry door always looked like it was about to fall. I know now that looking at an object kept me from thinking about my father. Each time I came to visit, I wondered with some anxiety whether the comforting sight of that grater might one day be erased. Without realizing it then, I appreciated the nuances of my family members and the constancy of their routines as an antidote to the absence of my deceased father.

This time together allowed the long morning to gradually blend into the dark afternoon with uninterrupted ease so that when the visit began and when it ended was unclear. There was no linear sense of time. The nuggets of melodramatic discord between Uncle Sal and Aunt Elvira, the passivity of Grandmother Sauline next to the laughter and arguing of children, and my mother's anxiety were the familiar scenes within that damp, musty home. Those visits grounded me in a world from which I had recently been uprooted. My relatives simultaneously authenticated my sense of incompleteness by at least representing some part of my father, and they filled me with a lasting wholeness that would enable me to absorb the shock of life's suffering to come.

I carried that feeling of special seclusion back to my home. It now felt less empty as I was able to relive those recent memories. I would make believe that all the relatives were living with me. Trying to recreate the coziness of my grandmother's kitchen, I often retreated to the far corner of our walk-in attic.

Pitched low, the ceiling was just high enough to allow me to crawl. After making my way through this narrow passage, a small atrium allowed me to stand. I had a feeling that every dark passage, no matter how threatening it appeared, would have the promise of freedom at the other end. The trip down the passage was a gauntlet of shadows; temptations to fear and anxiety always threatened my fragile equilibrium. Once I realized that the desire to go forward far outweighed the need to go back, I ignored the rows of hanging, ghost-like garments. (I would use this idea later on in life as a way of moving beyond the suffering).

At the end of the passage, on the floor of this dark and quiet space was a piece of hand-painted linoleum embossed with nursery rhyme figures and verse: this was a soothing, innocent reminder of child's play. This is the place where I read books, wrote letters, and had tea parties for my dolls. The memories of 74 Walnut Street taught me to paint each of my days as if it were a picture to be hung in a gallery. With a predetermined plan with a stroke of this and a splash of that, I would make moments to remember. Memories are more intense than the moment of reality in which they are born. My mind relishes the gift of life which I feel from the tone of voice, the glint in the eyes, the tilt of the head, or the nervous tap of a foot.

My father's death allowed me to appreciate that the moment at hand is a gift of opportunity. Through suffering, I have realized the joy that comes from the truth about loss. I sense that time is not abstract. It is concrete. It was recorded in Uncle Sal's date book. It was frozen in Aunt Elvira's paintings, and it was held in the last day that I saw my father in the open casket. Time is the sorrow that engraved gentle furrows on Grandmother's forehead, just as it was Uncle Sal's life savings frittered away in the stock market.

"We've had a good time."

"Come back soon, honey."

For, as I have experienced myself, it is our suffering, our broken heart that gives us insight into the suffering of others. Not pity, but sharing in the suffering ourselves because, we too, have known sorrow and loss. The extraordinary thing is that the insight of the heart is the magic that unleashes talents and potentialities within people that have been blocked as a result of their suffering.

Sufi Pir Vilayat

Pain

My first assignment on the surgical floor of the community hospital where I came to work was caring for Joe, who had sustained burns when his car caught fire. The flames melted his polyester suit against his body, causing his skin and the liquid polymers to bond. He had to be placed in a whirlpool tub so that the plastic could free itself from the skin.

Joe was a young man; only thirty-two. But you wouldn't know that to look at him. His face had a grey tone, and the redness of his eyes replaced the white. His face was wrinkled with lines of pain, and when I entered his room, he followed me with the look of a wild animal caught in a steel trap. Chained to a bed, unable to resume his life, and feeling the throbbing pain that was only intermittently relieved by injections of morphine, Joe's eyes were bottomless, dark pits of fear.

He watched me go about my task: first I placed my arms into the yellow, cotton, isolation gown, and then I placed a sterile glove on each hand while another nurse tied a surgical mask to my face. My eyes and his eyes followed each other, and I was never quite sure if he was looking at me, looking at him, or if he was just looking at me as a respite from his own hell. He could not speak because he had a tracheotomy tube in his airway. So, I studied the movement of his eyebrows in an attempt to read his pain. Seeking information from the speechless is like reading between the lines of poetry for meaning; the economy of words gives subtle clues for the reader to interpret. I needed to read Joe quickly and correctly. I watched his tortured face for signs to see if I was causing discomfort. An eyebrow tented in a high peak caused me to rethink my technique.

I sedated Joe so the application of ointment on the lower part of his body would not cause him more discomfort. My gloved hand applied a thick coating of silver nitrate cream to his exposed flesh. The skin surrounding the edge of the bums must still have had nerve function because when my hand touched a particularly tender area on the top of his thigh, his eyes rolled back and forth. A wild look came across his face, and he grabbed my wrist in a painfully firm grip. He wanted me to stop. I gave him as much morphine as the doctor would allow. But he still winced.

Although the morphine dulled his senses, Joe was still acutely aware that I was touching the raw, exposed skin. Joe was the victim, and he was dependent upon a stranger. I wondered if he hated this dependence or if he was thankful that I was his nurse. The longer I looked into Joe's quiet face, the more I found myself sinking into his bottomless pain. His pain became my struggle. As I accepted the reality of his human suffering, I became stunned like the swimmer taken down with the drowning victim; I had to fight for my own air.

I removed my eyes from the immediate situation by looking out the hospital's seventh-story window that was parallel to his body. I had to mix the moment beyond the room in an effort to blend the greater picture to the small part that I was encountering. The blue sky allowed a respite from the hell that I perceived. I needed to look at beauty in order to neutralize the painful truth. Despite the pain, there was joy here. With new strength, I turned my eyes to Joe who was sedated, and I continued his care. I tried to think of some other time as a way of staying with the moment. Paradoxically, the odor of his charred flesh reminded me of Girl Scout Camp.

I spent the summer I turned seven in Kent, Connecticut, at Camp Francis. The roaring open fire in the darkness shone upon twenty girls holding marshmallows on sticks. I could still feel the warm, embracing fire and smell the pungent stickiness of the marshmallows. I never realized that fire could be destructive. The memory of that odor brought me back to Joe's reality. This charred scent and the sight of his dark, piercing gaze touched me with such intensity that I ran out of the ward. In my innocence, I was not prepared to feel such rage. I did not know that someone else's suffering could be so subversive. My technique had failed.

At twenty and shaken, I wondered how I ever thought that I could be a nurse. My head felt dizzy from inhaling my own carbon dioxide. I tore the surgical mask off my face. My palms felt sweaty, my starched uniform uncomfortably close. I fled from the ward. The next day I asked for a new assignment.

Over the years, I've not just seen many other Joes, I have patiently endured their pain without rage. Their pain has not always come from the same source. Their ages have varied, and their backgrounds have all been different. I have fed babies born only to live momentarily due to the loss of a brain. Twenty years ago, I listened to a young man's profanities as he realized he was permanently paralyzed. One night, I sat at the edge of a man's bed while he desperately coped with news that his cancer had spread. While holding my hand, and nervously sobbing, he startled me.

At seventy, crying like a baby, Jerry lurched forward, and without permission kissed me on my right cheek. Why? Did he sense that I understood his anguish? Was it because I had given him a piece of my homemade apple pie the night before? Or, was it because, last week, I listened to his ramblings about being a self-made business man who had never had a formal education?

On another occasion, I saw a frail, bed-ridden man, open his eyes while he heard me tell his visitors about my first motorcycle ride. Hours later, this man who was dying, got out of bed and walked down a fifty-foot-long corridor to tell me how much he enjoyed the story because he too had experienced the thrill of motorcycle rides down the Catskill Mountains going eighty miles per hour. He hadn't thought of that pleasure until I reminded him. He walked back to his room and never rallied again. Someone else's story can color another's last moments of life.

Elizabeth is now eight. Recently, during a parent-teacher conference for her older sister, Elizabeth sat on my lap. The fifth-grade teacher looked at the two of us together. The teacher had never met Elizabeth before. The teacher did not say hello to Elizabeth, nor did she ask me Elizabeth's name. I don't know who felt more uncomfortable. I was appalled by this woman's lack of courtesy, yet she may have been appalled by a child who was more imperfect than herself. During the conference, Elizabeth turned to me and signed:

"I love you"

Elizabeth's Story

I NOW KNOW when I look at an elderly man sitting in a wheelchair, not to see an incapable human or his life as unfortunate. Instead, I see that the significance of his presence is the sum of his mannerisms that I choose to observe. I see the way he graciously flaps open his dinner napkin and places it on his lap. I watch his mouth slowly curl at the corners as a woman nears his view. I see his eyes brighten when someone sits down next to him. His eyes seem to glimmer with introspection as he listens to another. His smile widens, and together, these parts of his face brighten the room with an unspoken energy.

Sully, a retired "cop" from the Bronx, creates a lively environment in an otherwise dreary place. Each evening at six o'clock Sully sits in the comer of the dining room at the nursing home that I supervise. He is the resident entertainer. Creating a lively environment by placing his swing tapes into the recorder, this seemingly insignificant man is a bright spot for all of the other people of various ages, and differing disabilities.

Having met other people who shape their struggles into significant moments amidst their imperfect life gave me an opportunity to redefine the importance of every life. During my forty-third year, my passion for having a new child made me reflect further on the miracle of life, and the possibility, at my age, that I might carry a child with a disability.

As a nurse, I knew that statistically I was at a higher risk for carrying a child with Down syndrome. The medical facts were parlayed alongside my spiritual foundation. I believe that each life, having its own mystery, is meant to become part of other's lives. Each life has the profound potential of giving some life-altering insight for others. Meditating upon these thoughts, I spoke to my husband about the possibilities of another child, and together we agreed to enlarge our family of three. We also agreed not to have genetic testing because we were not going to agree to an abortion. Shortly after this discussion, I became pregnant.

When we broke the news of my pregnancy to our eldest son, twelve-year-old Jason became obsessed with negative thoughts. He knew that we were taking a risk and that we might have a child who would be emotionally taxing to care for. Jason wondered if I could handle this kind of child. There was not a day that went by when he did not needle me with probing questions. He asked me what I would do when people would stare at my funny-looking baby. He struggled with his role as an older brother. I had to deal with his anxieties, and at the same time, he forced me to think about issues I did not want to visit at such an early date. Of course, Jason did not know that families can be positively affected by the unique gifts of children with disabilities. Jason was constantly trying to predict the biography of this unborn child before she had a chance to live her own life. I finally pointed out to Jason that if I did have a child with challenges, everything would fall into place despite his doubts.

Months went by, and along with the stress from my son's anxieties, the pregnancy was unremarkable up until two weeks before the birth. At this point, I underwent a stress test. I was given fifteen grams of sugar while they checked to see if the baby jumped up and down in the womb. She didn't. My obstetrician sent me to the hospital for a sonogram of the fetal head and heart. The baby turned away from the doppler that's used to scan defects of the heart and brain. Each time the physician went to look at the heart, Elizabeth flipped over and showed her back, and when he looked at the back of the skull for the extra skin fold indicative of a Down syndrome trait, she turned her head in the opposite direction. The physician never saw such an uncooperative baby. He never saw what he was looking for. It was to be a mystery.

My delivery was induced a week early because of the inability to diagnose why the stress test didn't excite the baby. After an hour, the baby girl was delivered naturally without drugs. She was placed on my abdomen for inspection. I was the first to notice her condition. Although her face was symmetrical and beautiful, her eyes were subtly turned up at the corners. I said in a soft voice: "She has Down syndrome." Suddenly the staff became hyper alert and defensive: they inspected her mouth and listened to her heart, looking for clefts and septal defects. They asked, "How do you know this?" I said, "The shape of her eyes is different from the eyes of my other children."

Elizabeth was not in my arms more than two hours when it became apparent that her heart wasn't going to close off from the maternal circulation. I had never experienced any of my babies having to be whisked off by the paramedics to another hospital in an Isolette. On medical advice, I could not accompany Elizabeth. While on bed rest, miles away, I feared for her life and felt empty as though part of me was missing. I felt as if she had been abducted. In an effort to cope, I tried to cloak her absence in some grandiose, beatific thought, *there goes my special baby who will touch the lives of all those who see her.*

As I encapsulated myself into this self-made solace that escalated into an intermittent emotional high, I felt both excited and afraid. I had never experienced mothering a child with physical delays. Probably due to the post-traumatic stress, several ideas with a similar theme crossed my mind like photo flashes that blinded me with insightful clarity. I began to doubt my emotional strength for the plight ahead. I meditated on the value of accepting the perfection within what outwardly may appear to be imperfect, but I was equally perplexed with the fear of the unknown. I found myself breathing in and out with controlled deep breaths like I did when I was giving birth. It is one thing to say that I believe in something, and it is totally different to actually live with the challenges of that belief.

Confronted with a new responsibility, I found myself feeling pity, insecurity, and a sense of failure. I was to mother a child who would be dependent upon me and the family for the rest of her life. My strong body felt like cotton candy without the cone in the center that holds all the delicately spun threads together. The core of my being was a foundation built on faith that I had learned from accepting the other struggles. I was at the end of myself looking inward with deep examination and with utter exhaustion. No more games, no answers from the specialists, no one saying it will be alright. No God saying it will be easy. I was looking at myself with more reflection than what a mirror could provide. The naked truth was my fear threatened to eat me alive, and I had to survive this. Just then, my husband came to pick me up for the hour-long drive to see Elizabeth in the intensive care unit at Yale Children's Hospital.

Leaving my other children at home, and only knowing the experience of the well-baby, I was a novice mother totally led by Elizabeth. When I arrived at her side, I felt a sudden surge of strength. Moving toward her, I lifted the lid of the Isolette and went to work busily swaddling my baby in a receiving blanket with her two intravenous lines and the oxygen tubing. She could not suck because her mouth muscles were weak, so I had to deliver my milk in a bottle that was dribbled into her mouth. She gazed into my eyes intently as I sensed a transformation within myself: I felt an immediate surge of innate strength, an unequivocal desire to advocate for my new baby. In a tight bond of longing for the right thoughts to turn this atypical experience into typical one, I began to look around at the other babies in the neonatal intensive care unit. Standing there, as her mother, and knowing the mental delays that Elizabeth would endure for the rest of her life, I held her soft cheek up to my lips. With unconditional love, I kissed her repeatedly. She was my baby, a gift. Her differences paled in significance to the fact that she was alive and doing well.

As I looked around at the other infants, some of whom were born without vital organs, my baby's needs suddenly seemed lighter. I sensed urgency in the faces of the other parents. One parent of a perfectly attractive boy told me her son, born without a pancreas, was awaiting a transplant operation that had never been done before. She asked me how I had the strength to accept my baby's condition, and I said: "She will have delays, but her delays will teach the rest of us patience." There was an irony in that mother's perception of one imperfection being heavier than another. Her baby was about to undergo a life-threatening procedure with a poor prognosis, where my baby was going to hop, skip, and jump just a little later than everyone else. I was beginning to understand how the world was about to perceive Elizabeth, and I was aware of the need to witness my unconditional love to a child that others would perceive as unfortunate.

What happened after that moment of enlightenment has been happening to me ever since Elizabeth was born. I have been experiencing life from a totally different angle. Previously, I had perceived events as joyful or sad, but after her birth, those perceptions have changed. I see differing degrees of struggles to be opportunities for self-enlighten-ment. I am hyper alert to the value of those lives around me, or to the potential of those I may never meet. Every struggle seems to either make people emotionally stronger, or weaker. Yet, in my life, there seems to be a direct proportion: the more intense the struggle, the more able I have become to accept and live through the next struggle. I live in the moment and the moment is what it is.

I accept the beauty in Elizabeth's persistence to learn. Her commitment has more value than money. When other children whine for more gifts during Christmas, I look at Elizabeth who is content in having a single present. When I see Elizabeth teaching herself not to do a behavior by literally telling herself "no," I think that her methods of learning make more sense. Without restraint, Elizabeth dances to music with undaunted ease, while the rest of us would need a few glasses of wine to be so uninhibited. She is what she is, and that is great. Because I have seen Elizabeth reach her pinnacles of success with lengthy periods of delay, I see the indomitable spirit that moves her in her own timeline of success.

I know that it is better to accept what is unchangeable, and that the only thing I can change is my perspective—one which can be negative and draining, or positive and uplifting. The seriousness of a situation exists, but it can be buffered with humor. When I want to give up on a project that needs my strength and endurance, I look over at Elizabeth spending patient, unbroken moments imitating her sister's speech. When I see Elizabeth holding a book as she mimics the action of a typical six-year-old, I understand more fully the meaning of undying effort, simple joy, and truth. When I am not empathetic to the misery of another because I am caught up in my own misery, I see Elizabeth extending beyond her less-than-average-IQ with honest empathy as she pats the arms of an elderly person.

In her own way, Elizabeth engages with the world around her. As she quickens at the cry of a baby and shows quiet concern, I am reminded that the value of her life lies in the empathy that she shows to the rest of us. Although Jason continued to struggle with Elizabeth's developmental delays, I finally told him that she would thrive despite his speculations and doubts. I told him that if one of his sixteen-year-old-friends wrapped himself around a tree and sustained traumatic brain damage, he would not make fun of him, nor would he, as a friend, love him any less. Jason's misgivings made me articulate thoughts that I would not have been so eloquently able to produce had he not forced them from my lips in order to quiet his anxieties. Jason's need to test my acceptance of Elizabeth helped me to prove to myself that I was quite capable of accepting the honor of being Elizabeth's lifetime advocate.

Jason's doubts and Elizabeth's will to live allow me to act on my convictions. 1 truly believed in what I had learned. I was re-renewed. I explained to Jason, and simultaneously to myself, that society affects the way we judge people. Society gives us one notion of perfection, and by comparison to a standard, we discard all of the people who fail to measure up to that standard. A child born into a family is a vital member of that family, and the very fact that a child, any child, makes it into this world and thrives is itself an example of perfection. Furthermore, Elizabeth is not less perfect for being more fully and uniquely herself, any more than any other person.

To this observer, one's life is not a tally score of one's weaknesses, nor is it a series of unfortunate events measured according to someone's set of standards. Therefore, when I see Elizabeth, my mind does not dwell on her aberrant, chromosomal arrangement. I don't worry about her need to be dependent on others. I do appreciate that her life has been a gift to her family, her friends, and her teachers. Elizabeth's life rearranges our way of perceiving her greatness.

Elizabeth's wholeness is a composite of her nuances: it's in her smile, her ability to straighten out the family's shoes in one perfect line, and the empathy she shows toward her sister. To all of us, she appears whole.

PART TWO:
ACADEMIC REFLECTIONS

IN THE MEMOIR concerning her mother's secret world of epilepsy, *Other People's Secrets,* memoirist Patricia Hampl frames her essay with unresolved guilt and detached determination. Since her mother was ashamed of an illness that caused her body to jump and twitch in public, Patricia became ashamed as well. Hampl writes her memoir so she can understand her mother's pain and to bring an adult perspective to her own childhood.

After reading this memoir, I became more sensitive to the people in my pieces. I made separate entries about their possible perspectives, and on some occasions, I contacted the people involved, both to interview them and to obtain permission for publication. During the interviews, I became aware that my ego guided my writing, so as I compared our different perspectives, I realized the need to edit my pieces. As I revised, I was fearful that I might lose the creative style that began each piece.

On the Form of the Essay

The form of Benjamin Franklin's essay, "Developing the First Public Library," allowed me to see the germ of his idea in the first paragraph. In his clear and simple introduction, he wrote with a personal reflection, which gives the reader a glimpse of the passion behind the essay. This passion holds the essay together. I was immediately impressed by his style. The reading caused me to stop and write my essay, "My Father's Funeral." Very naturally, I became more acutely aware of my writing process and my need to balance insights with facts. I constructed the essay as a dance pattern between the brain and the heart, between facts and emotion. The end result was an essay in which each paragraph begins with an emotional line that is carried along with facts, which end in a reflective note that marks a transition into the next paragraph's emotional introduction. Having a visual pattern of facts and emotions kept me anchored where, otherwise, I would tend to float away on an abstract tributary.

On Secondary Sources within One's Memoir

Andrew Hudgins begins his memoir reflection, "Half Answered Prayers," with the words, "when I was a child." Hudgins remembers praying anxiously to God for material

objects. His desire was not only to receive those posses-
sions, but also to prove that God hears and delivers, that
God is authentic. As he moved from his late teens into
his middle twenties, Hudgins declared himself agnostic,
or perhaps even an atheist, but he never stopped praying.
Although he remembered himself as a child lying in bed
at night, spending countless hours pleading for a tran-
sistor radio, he criticized his shallowness from an adult
perspective. As that author penned the memory, he recalls
with wisdom, "Even then, years before I could envision
terminal cancer patients praying frantically for a miracle cure, and years before I read of Jews in Nazi death
camps beseeching God for justice, I knew that asking for
a radio ... was ignoble" (340). The memoirist has the awe-
some responsibility of not only envisioning the past from
one stage of development while writing about it from
another stage of development, but also of taking care not
to change a childhood memory to fit an adult perspective.

In the final draft of my piece, "The Tree House," I ret-
rospectively placed thoughts to support a thesis. This final
carving out of words while replacing others distorted the
memory. Where I originally wrote from a child's perspective, at a later date I wrote from an adult perspective, and
in doing so, I lost my child-like stance. It would have been
more believable if I had written both perspectives in the
original draft; however, I read Hudgin's piece during that

final edit and was able to bring both perspectives together. This dual perspective illuminates the mechanism of recollection: the adult validates immaturity with adult wisdom. The last half of Hudgin's essay is devoted to the author's developing sense of spirituality, including his continuous sense of doubt. He declares that his prayers are both centripetal and centrifugal, directed both inward and outward. He weaves in T. S. Eliot's "East Coker" to illustrate a point that effective communication is based on word choice, honesty, and tone.

After reading this personal essay, I noted how the richness of the piece is enhanced by secondary sources. The reader receives more input from other disciplines, and these nuances may stimulate more thought and secure a better understanding of the piece as a whole. This was especially meaningful to me during the early draft of my essay, "Faded Photograph." As I wrote the piece, I intermittently read the following authors for intertextual ideas: Nabokov, David Bohrn, John Briggs, Marcel Proust, Shakespeare, and Virginia Woolf.

The Influence of the Southern Accent upon My Writing Style

In my search for nuances, I browsed the work of Tennessee Williams, and while reading the play "A Streetcar Named

Desire,"1 was influenced by the cadence of his southern accent. The syntax caused me to speak the words with the same accent, and I began to write my essay, "Faded Photograph," with more elongated sentences that had a similar beat. The result was organic: my sentence structure blossomed. I found that the southern voice articulates the main idea by richly supporting it with colorful clues. The numerous uses of subordinate clauses and parallelisms helped me form a movement that both quantified and qualified my main idea.

With further investigation, I soon realized that other notable southern writers also influenced my writing. My sentences expanded with qualifying clues that made my central idea more vivid, three-dimensional and visual. Plays, novels, and short stories, written by southern writers, eased my tendency to edit my voice. As a writer, I was embarrassed to reveal myself fully in "My Father's Funeral"; however, when I read Toni Morrison's *Sula,* written in a Southern voice, I experienced that the revelation of an author's feelings offers the opportunity to fully exchange empathy between the reader and the writer. As I began the first draft of "Elizabeth," I felt that not only was it acceptable to share truthful transparency, but it was also, for me, an invitation to be fearlessly open with the reader. Morrison's elaboration on complex connotations loosen into luxurious layers of thought whereby the main idea blossoms like an unfolding peony. I became acutely aware of my own tight thoughts: I realized that when I economize my sentences in fear that I might lose my original thought, I become tangential. Now, when I enjoy writing for the sheer thrill of communicating my idea to the reader, I discipline my brain to logically portray my heart. I write with authority because I am the writer who forms the words, and I am responsible for drawing conclusions, making analogies, and inventing new ideas.

Creative Writing and Science

In *Science Order and Creativity,* authors David Bohm and F. David Peat, regard the creation of metaphor as a way for the brain to enter a very perceptive state of great energy and passion, "in which some of the excessively rigid aspects of the tacit infrastructure are bypassed or dissolved" (61). They go on to say that what results is a new understanding of one entity brought about by comparing it with another very different entity (61)."

My writings are based on metaphorical connections that will appeal to the reader. In this side-by-side dance of similarities and contrasts, I strengthen my arguments and clarify my main point with other experiences (e.g., the "Pain" essay) that I have had. This conjoining of memories prevents me from coming up with one point of reference. What happens is an enfolding or layering of similar ideas until a fuller clarity is achieved. These metaphorical connections overlap, connect, intercede, and portray one thought based on many others. This interpolation of ideas is similar to the collection of secondary references that a researcher would be expected to have in a well-thought-out paper.

The International Voice and the Effect on My Voice

I read the short stories of Frank O'Connor because these fictions are transparently autobiographical. As the omniscient narrator, he transcribes his own viewpoints and gives the reader the proof of his insight: "But even then, some unfamiliar feeling was stirring at her heart, she felt she was losing control of herself, and was being moved about like a chessman" (663). Looking at this description of detailed emotion added a layer of dimension to my own style.

Where it would be difficult to capture this feeling, O'Connor's words show a simple clarity about an abstract idea. He goes on to say that the feeling was so light, that it led her aimlessly along, and yet was so great a force that it shook her from head to foot (662). O'Connor's description of people goes beyond the physical as he explores the connection behind appearances: "She was tongue-tied, twisted, and unhappy. She had a curious raw, almost timid smile as though she felt people desired no better sport than hurting her' (l 03). This description reinforced my need for authority in my voice as I reflected upon and rewrote "Elizabeth." When other people questioned my martyr-like acceptance of a special child, I realized that my main point was lost within my own sense of drama. I was challenged by their misinterpretation of my sincerity. I almost threw the piece away, thinking it was a reflection of my ego. Then I took hold of myself and rewrote the piece with my original intention, which was to portray an awareness of what I learned from having a challenged-child.

On Reading about Similar Experiences

I read James's Baldwin's *Notes of a Native Son* after I wrote "My Father's Funeral." Baldwin's words reaffirmed the appropriateness of my memory when he says,

> For my father's funeral, I had nothing black to wear and this posed a nagging problem all day long. It was one of those problems, simple, or impossible of solution, to which the mind insanely

clings in order to avoid the mind's real trouble (232)

Here I realized that writing memoirs is a brave act, one that demands not only total concentration as the writer remains in the present while leaping into another time zone, but also an act that exposes the writer. Once the writer is exposed, there is an untold series of unplanned, involuntary emotional reactions, whereby the ego tries to hide the painful reality. Baldwin spoke about children at his father's funeral, and I got a glimpse of what I must have looked like as a child when he said, "But there is also something very gallant about children at such moments. It has something to do with their silence and gravity and with the fact that one cannot help them. Their legs, somehow, seem exposed, so that it is at once incredible and terribly clear that their legs are all they have to hold them up" (235). After I read these lines, I looked at my own recollection as an adult writing about my feelings as a child. I recognized Baldwin's insight in my own work. The similarities of our childhood experiences made me compare our writing techniques. Where I had written, "My head started to feel achy, my thoughts became distant-swirling in a vortex of disbelief, emptiness, and hopelessness—my knees buckled under me as I stood up" ("My

Father's Funeral"), my imagistically-implied agony was similar to that described by Baldwin. I felt validated.

On Reading Another Writer's Diary

Virginia Woolf's, *A Writer's Diary*, inspired me to write memoirs. By reading her words, I was reassured that what I was doing was not only important, but difficult too. Having read about her fears and frustrations allowed me to own my own. In early stages of my writings, my feelings were put aside so that I could move on. What made it difficult to move at a steady pace was that the repression of feelings would eventually release when I least expected it, and several times, I was overcome with tears. I was temporarily blinded by the sting of saline-soaked eyes. Woolf s testimony gave me words with which to encompass my feelings. Journaling, she wrote: "Four months of work, and heaven knows how much reading—not of an exalted kind either—and I cannot see how to make anything of it" (185). Her steady self-criticism made me aware that I was not alone in my own. At one point, she says she had to stop editing and changing the text because it was time. During the whole writing process, I would find myself sitting on the tip of my chair with my toes pointed on the floor like a cougar ready to pounce on the paper. I was frozen in fear that some force would keep me from finishing my thought or that my flow would be interrupted—never be reclaimed again.

There is some high exhilaration about writing from memory: it is that moment that the mind curls itself from the present against the backbone of the past. This curling and enfolding of the mind is elicited in Woolf's fiction, a fiction that is so completely realistic it might as well be her memoir. In *To the Lighthouse,* the character Mrs. Ramsey comments on life:

> She looked at life, for she had a clear sense of it here, something real, something private, which she shared neither with children, nor with her husband. A sort of transaction went on between them, in which she was on one side, and life was on another. (58–60)

This piece of fiction represented for me a conduit of empathy between Woolf's persona and the reader. Specifically, when I had originally wanted to write an essay about my grandmother's apartment, I found the task too overwhelming and my prose too unclear. Woolf's tendency to weave nuances into concrete objects influenced my fluid writing style. Relaxed at the end of my pieces, I then devoted what I learned of style to the piece called

"Faded Photographs." It was at this time that I wrote my best work, and I attribute it to the end of this writing journey. As I read other works, and wrote more volume, I grew as a writer. As I developed a voice, a pattern emerged, and I became not only aware of myself as a writer, but also I respected myself for carrying out this writing.

When I read Nabokov's *Speak Memory,* I was left with a unique notion of time. I decided to embellish my essay "Faded Photographs" after reading this passage: "I confess I do not believe in time. I like to fold my magic carpet, after use, in such a way as to superimpose one part of the pattern upon another" (138). It is with great ease that a word or a phrase will invite my own whirlwind of thoughts, or, in reverse, I will write a story and then pick up a book randomly only to find an exact line that sums up what I have said in my own work.

Finding him was like finding a friend who enjoys writing memoirs, and to read his voice was the final nudge, that affirmation, that urges us all to tell our stories. I finished my essay with Nabokov's lines, though I found them after I had completed my work. Finding words to match my sentiment caused an epiphany. Where he wrote, "I have journeyed back in thought—with thought hopelessly tapering off as I went to remote regions where I groped for some secret outlet only to discover that the prison of time is spherical" (291), I became more engaged with the abstractness of time.

Nabokov spoke to me at a time when I was consumed with writing these autobiographical pieces. As my task became both sweeter and more complex, his words were reassuring: "It is one thing to conceive the main play of a composition and another to construct it" (290). Then again, sometimes when I surprise myself at the rapid fluidity of my memories, it seems as though, without even thinking about writing, my ideas take on a life of their own, prompting me to write them down. Because the memories are my own, I never expect that others will have the same experiences or express them in quite the same way. I am always taken aback when I see the style of another memoir. When I write, I do not intentionally have a prefabricated form; in fact, if I did, it might force my thoughts into an unnatural discourse. Each essay takes its own shape from the urgency of the passion behind my memory. Other factors shape the paragraphs, such as distractions while I write or time limitations. One day I had the gift of four uninterrupted hours at a bookstore where I sat surrounded by many of the books I have listed here. While browsing in the works of various authors, I found several quotations that could quite easily fit my own essays. I was shocked at the ease with which these quotes surfaced, and how appropriately they fit my essays, like that last, lost piece of the puzzle.

WORKS CITED AND CONSULTED

Adams, Hazard, Leroy Searle. *Critical Theory Since 1965*. Florida: University Presses of Florida, 1986.

Auslander, Joseph. *The Sonnets of Petrach*. New York: Longmans, Green & Co, 1931.

Baldwin, James. "Notes of a Native Son." Oates and Atwan 220–238.

Bell, Quentin. Ed Anne Oliver Bell. *The Diary of Virginia Woolf.* New York: Harvest Press, 1982.

Bourne, Randolph. "The Handicapped." Ed. Oates and Atwan, 57–70.

Briggs, John. *Fire in the Crucible*. Michigan: Phanes Press, 2000.

Didion, Joan. *Why I Write.* "New York Times Book Review." 9 Dec. 1976: 22. Rpt. in *The Writer on Her Work.* Ed. Janet Stemburg. New York: Norton, 1980.

Eggers, Dave. *A Heartbreaking Work of Staggering Genius.* New York: Random House, 2001.

Henderson, Bill. *The Pushcart Prize 2001 XXV,* New York: Pushcart Press, 2201.

Hudgins, Andrew. "Half Answered Prayers." Henderson, 340–355.

Hurston, Zora Neale. "How It Feels to Be Colored Me." Oates and Atwan, 114–117.

Joyce, James. *The Dubliners.* Viking, New York: Viking Press, 1976.

Jung, C. G. *Memories, Dreams, Reflections.* Ed. Aniela Jaffe, Trans. Richard and Clara Winston. New York: Vintage, 1989.

Kimbrough, Robert, ed. "Astrophel and Stella" *Sir Philip Sidney Selected Prose and Poetry.* UP Wisconsin, 1983.

Leaska, Mitchell. *The Virginia Woolf Reader.* New York: Harcourt Brace & Co., NY, 1984.

Lewis, C. S. *The Four Loves.* New York: Harcourt Brace & Co., 1960.

McCabe, Nancy. "The End of the Tunnel." Henderson, 468–479.

McCullers, Carson. *Collected Stories.* Houghton Mifflin & Co., I 987.

Oates, Joyce Carol and Robert Atwan, eds. *The Best American Essay of the Century.* New York: Houghton Mifflin & Co., 2000.

___. "They All Just Went Away." Oates and Atwan, 553–563.

O'Connor, Flannery. "Good Country People." *A Good Man Is Hard to Find and Other Stories*.

New York: Harcourt Brace & Co., 1955.

Nabokov, Vladimir. "Perfect Past." Oates and Atwan, 303–312.

___. *Speak Memory: An Autobiography Revisited.* New York: Random House, 1967.

O'Casey, Sean. *Three Plays.* New York: St. Martin's Press, 1926.

O'Connor, Frank. *Collected Stories.* New York: Random House, 1931.

Pirsig, Robert M. *Zen and the Art of Motorcycle Maintenance.* New York: Bantam, 1975.

Primadi, Diane. *Recollections of My Life as a Woman.* New York: Penguin, 2001.

Proust, Marcel. "Regrets, Reveries the Color of Time." *The Complete Short Stories of Marcel Proust.* Trans. Joachim Neugroschel. New York: Cooper Square Press, 2001.

Ross, W. D. *Aristotle—Great Books.* Chicago University Press, 1952.

Welty, Eudora. "A Sweet Devouring." Oates and Atwan 246–251.

Williams, Tennessee. *A Streetcar Named Desire.* New York: Penguin, 1927.

Winterson, Jeanette. *Written on the Body.* New York: Random House, 1994.

Woolf, Virginia. *To the Lighthouse.* New York: Harcourt Brace & Co., 1972.

_____. *A Writer's Diary.* Ed. Leonard Woolf. New York: Harcourt Brace & Co., 1934.

_____. "The Humane Art." *The Death of the Moth and Other Essays.* New York: Harcourt Brace, NY 1942.

_____. *A Room of One's Own.* Harcourt Brace & Co., 1929.

Yeats, William Butler. *Selected Poems and Three Plays,* Ed. M. L. Rosenthal. New York: Macmillan & Co., 1986.